W9-ANM-405

DATE DUE

472859

598.8
KOT

Kottke, Jan.

From egg to robin

H.C. STORM SCHOOL
BATAVIA, IL 60510

606239 00896          38539D          003

# From Egg to Robin

By Jan Kottke

Children's Press
A Division of Grolier Publishing
New York / London / Hong Kong / Sydney
Danbury, Connecticut

Photo Credits: Cover and all photos © Dwight Kuhn
Contributing Editors: Mark Beyer and Eliza Berkowitz
Book Design: MaryJane Wojciechowski

Library of Congress Cataloging-in-Publication Data

Kottke, Jan.
    From egg to robin / by Jan Kottke.
        p. cm. — (How things grow)
    Includes bibliographical references and index.
    Summary: Simple text and photographs show how an egg becomes a robin.
    ISBN 0-516-23308-4 (lib. bdg.) — ISBN 0-516-23508-7 (pbk.)
    1. Robins—Life cycles—Juvenile literature. [1. Robins. 2. Animals—Infancy.] I. Title.
QL696.P288 K68 2000
    598.8'42—dc21
                                                        00-024378

Copyright © 2000 by Rosen Book Works, Inc.
All rights reserved. Published simultaneously in Canada.
Printed in the United States of America.
    12 13 14 15 16 17 18 19 20 R 14 13 12 11 10 09 08 07 06

# Contents

Robin **eggs** are laid in a **nest**.

The eggs are bright blue.

The mother sits on the eggs to keep them warm.

7

The robin eggs have **hatched**.

The baby birds are very small.

9

The mother brings food for the baby birds.

The baby robins open their mouths wide.

11

H.C. STORM SCHOOL

The baby robins start to grow feathers.

The feathers keep them warm.

12

13

The baby birds grow larger.

Now they have more feathers.

They still live in the nest.

15

It's time to learn how to fly.

A baby robin flaps its wings to **practice**.

17

This baby robin has grown up.

It looks like its mother.

The robin can take care of itself.

19

The grown robin now has babies of its own.

It brings food to them so they can grow.

21

# New Words

**eggs** (**ehgz**) an object that holds a growing animal

**hatched** (**hacht**) came out of an egg

**nest** (**nehst**) a bird's home made out of sticks and twigs

**practice** (**prac**-tis) to do something many times

# To Find Out More

**Books**
*Baby Bird*
by Joyce Dunbar
Candlewick Press

*The Robins in Your Backyard*
by Nancy Carol Willis
Bird Song Books

**Web Sites**
**The Life of Birds**
http://www.pbs.org/lifeofbirds
This site has a lot of news about birds. Learn more about baby birds and find out how birds are able to sing.

**Natural History Notebooks**
http://www.nature.ca/notebooks/english/mon2.htm
Here you will learn about many different kinds of animals, including birds. See pictures of robins and learn more about them.

# Index

About the Author

Jan Kottke is the owner/director of several preschools in the Tidewater area of Virginia. A lifelong early education professional, she is completing a phonics reading series for preschoolers.

Reading Consultants

Kris Flynn, Coordinator, Small School District Literacy, The San Diego County Office of Education

Shelly Forys, Certified Reading Recovery Specialist, W.J. Zahnow Elementary School, Waterloo, IL

Peggy McNamara, Professor, Bank Street College of Education, Reading and Literacy Program

24